Evidence for Special Creation
and a Young Earth

Evidence for Special Creation and a Young Earth

Articles collected by Kathleen Dunn, who also wrote commentary.

Thanks and appreciation to my husband, Tom, my encourager and sounding board.

Table of Contents

Introduction

Most of us grew up believing that the earth is billions of years old—that is what we were taught in our science classes; and whether we believed it or not, we were told that we shared a common ancestor with the apes. There is so much written about the topic of undirected evolution, and it is so widely taught in schools, that we assume the information we have received is factual. However, in the face of studies that have shown chance evolution to be untenable, it may be time to question the rationale for textbooks to continue to publish unproven theory as if it were fact and for scientists to continue to embrace it. Perhaps the scientific community holds on to flawed theories for philosophical and religious reasons, as protection from observations which may point to an intelligent Designer.

According to Dr. George Wald, who won the Nobel Prize in 1967 for his studies on the function of the human eye:

"When it comes to the origin of life there are only two possibilities: creation or spontaneous generation. There is no 3rd way. Spontaneous

generation was disproved 100 years ago, but that leads us to only one other conclusion, that of supernatural creation. We cannot accept that on philosophical grounds; therefore, we choose to believe the impossible: that life arose spontaneously by chance!"
George Wald, PhD, "The Origin Of Life," *Scientific American*, August 1954, Vol. 191, No. 2, https://www.jstor.org/stable/e24943585

I have discovered that the science which points to special creation is strong and cohesive, with supporting data which cannot be explained by random accident. I had never heard about creation science until 1990 when I was already an adult. There had always been a disconnect for me, because it was hard to reconcile what was presented in my science classes with my faith. I had always believed that the Genesis account of creation was inspired, however, science classes taught us that the earth was billions of years old and that over time chemicals came together to form plants and animals and eventually human beings. Fossils were dated by the rocks in which they were found, and the rocks were dated by the fossils they contained; a circular type of logic.

I can remember almost falling out of my chair with wonder and excitement the first time I heard a scientist lecture on the great flood and how it had changed the earth. A few years later I attended a series of lectures by Dr. Walt Brown, a retired Air Force colonel and Chief of Science and Technology with the U.S. Air Force—Dr. Brown had been a National Science Foundation Fellow, and he received his doctorate in mechanical engineering from MIT. He said he had never questioned the theory of evolution early in his career and had reconciled his faith with the idea of theistic evolution—the idea that God could have directed evolution. However, through science he discovered many flaws in the theory of evolution, and upon retirement, he opened the Center for Scientific Creation. His book, *In the Beginning*, is now in its 8th edition. I sat spellbound as he explained various methods for dating the earth, discredited artists' sketches of prehistoric man, and used a test tube filled with sand, shells, and water to demonstrate how the global flood had triggered a rapid burial of the prehistoric world. He was able to address questions regarding the flood, the formation of the Grand Canyon, comets, global warming, and so much more—the science seemed to be cohesive.

Over the years I have read countless books which affirm creation science—it surprises me that many people are not even aware of its existence or the strong evidence which supports the Biblical narrative found in Genesis and referenced in numerous accounts in both the Old and New Testaments. I am not a scientist by educational training, but like most thoughtful literate people, I can appreciate the scientific facts and discoveries that are explained in textbooks, periodicals and creation science books, typically written for the non-scientist. I will refer to many of the books as well as articles on specific studies. Please note that each book typically contains many references and footnotes which can take you on many investigative journeys. Also note that there is a wide range of thought and expertise among the various scientists.

It is important to acknowledge that even though theories may be called "science," there is a difference between observable science and speculation. According to Encyclopedia Britannica, "In a typical application of the scientific method, a researcher develops a hypothesis, tests it through various means, and then modifies the hypothesis on the basis of the outcome of the tests and experiments. The modified hypothesis is then retested, further modified, and tested again, until it becomes consistent with observed phenomena and testing outcomes." By gathering consistent reliable data, scientists develop theories.

The leading explanation for the formation of the universe is the big bang theory, which claims that over 13.8 billion years the cosmos has been expanding, and that over the course of time various particles such as neutrons and electrons have collided in such a way that eventually planets and stars were formed. In time life sprang forth, starting with microorganisms, which ultimately evolved into human beings.

Dr. Brown states, "The big bang theory, now known to be seriously flawed, was based on three observations: the redshift of light from distant stars, the cosmic microwave background radiation (CMB), and the amount of helium in the universe. All three have been poorly misunderstood." He continues to explain that if the universe were expanding, increasing the potential energy of stars and galaxies with no corresponding loss of energy elsewhere, it would violate the law of conservation of energy.

He states that if the big bang had happened, distant galaxies should be decelerating, but measurements show that the expansion of the universe is speeding up. Further, the big bang theory does not explain CMB or the amount of helium in the universe. Dr. Brown devotes several pages to the theory in his book, *In the Beginning*, which can also be accessed on the internet at *www.creationscience.com*.

Note that the big bang theory is inconsistent with chaos theory, as defined by *New Scientist*; "Chaos [t]heory presents a universe that is deterministic, obeying fundamental physical laws, but with a predisposition for disorder, complexity, and unpredictability." In other words, in the observable world, living things tend to break down over time.

In contrast, using the "scientific method," creation scientists can point to indisputable intelligent design. In his book, *Signature in the Cell*, Dr. Stephen Meyer points out that fully functioning systems need to be in place to sustain life. In addition, the atmospheric conditions would have to be dialed to a very precise range. The "primordial soup," which would contain the elements needed for life to begin, is unlikely to have ever existed. A living cell contains 20 essential amino acids. Each of the amino acids would have to be produced by chance and then line up next to one another—also by chance. Since the earth's atmosphere contains about 21% oxygen, the oxidation process would be destructive to biomolecules not contained within a cell. Further, geological data indicates that oxygen in the earth's atmosphere has always been similar to its current condition. The data used in countless pertinent studies does follow scientific methodology; it is observable and consistent.

In chapter 4 of *Signature in the Cell*, Meyer explains that the structure of proteins depends on the arrangement of its amino acids. The question posed to us is what determines that arrangement? In chapter 5 Meyer notes that information is worthless without a system which can process it, and only whole cells contain all the machinery needed for self-replication. The translation of the code needs more than 100 functioning macromolecular components, which themselves are coded in the DNA. Meyer goes on to state that the production of proteins requires DNA, but the production of DNA requires proteins. Additionally, the cells require specific enzymes—the processes are complicated.

Meyer wrote that the probability of a random process producing a sequenced chain of amino acids was around one in ten to the 63rd power—about the same chance as finding a single marked atom out of all the atoms in our galaxy via a blind undirected search!

Meyer had an opportunity to interview Nobel Prize winning physicist Eugene Wigner at a conference at Yale. When Meyer asked him about the origin of life problem, he explained why he thought that "the odds are overwhelmingly against any process of undirected chemical evolution producing life." Meyer, Stephen, PhD, *Signature in the Cell*, 2009, pp. 141, 211

(*There is a cartoon I love in which the professor states, "Hydrogen is a colorless, odorless gas, which if given enough time, turns into people."* An analogy which brings chance into perspective is the story about a tornado circulating through a junk yard and, after a long time, a fully functional 747 jet appears–tray tables and seat belts in place.)

Charles Darwin, who is considered the father of evolutionary theory, did not have a sophisticated understanding of biochemistry—functions which take place within the cell. Scientists in his day knew that organisms were made up of cells, but they did not have equipment to observe processes which go on within the cell or how one cell would communicate with another. In other words, his understanding was incomplete and simplistic.

"Biochemistry has demonstrated that any biological apparatus involving more than one cell (such as an organ or a tissue) is necessarily an intricate web of many different, identifiable systems of horrendous complexity. The 'simplest' self-sufficient, replicating cell has the capacity to produce thousands of different proteins and other molecules, at different times and under variable conditions. Synthesis, degradation, energy generation, replication, repair, communication—all of these functions take place in virtually every cell, and each function itself requires the interaction of numerous parts."
Michael J. Behe, PhD, *Darwin's Black Box*, p. 46

"Before the evolutionary process of building the first cell could begin, a diverse array of key

molecules would have to be magically generated in some primordial matrix or soup. Such molecules would have to include various amino acids, pyrimidines, purines, lipids, and sugars. The alleged spontaneous generation of these key building blocks in the proper forms and amounts is an impossible hurdle. Putting these basic molecules together via naturalistic processes into larger chains and structures containing the vital molecular information needed for life is also impossible!"
Jeffrey P. Tomkins, PhD, "The Impossibility of Life's Evolutionary Beginnings," *Acts and Facts*, February 28, 2018, https://www.icr.org/article/impossibility-lifes-evolutionary-beginnings

"'Scientists,' the physicist Paul Davies has observed, 'are slowly waking up to an inconvenient truth–the universe looks suspiciously like a fix. The issue concerns the very laws of nature themselves. For 40 years, physicists and cosmologists have been quietly collecting examples of all too convenient coincidences and special features in the underlying laws of the universe that seem to be necessary in order for life, and hence conscious beings, to exist. Change any one of them and

the consequences would be lethal.'"
David Berlinski, *The Devil's Delusion*, pp. 110-111

According to Francis Crick, "An honest man, armed with all the knowledge available to us now, could only state that in some sense, the origin of life appears to be at the moment to be almost a miracle, so many are the conditions which would have had to have been satisfied to get it going."
Francis Crick, PhD, *Life Itself: Its Origin and Nature*, p. 81

Significantly, Charles Darwin, in his book *On Origin of Species*, makes no mention of any experimental research, nor does the book contain any mathematical calculations.

"Despite huge gaps in the fossil evidence, and though he lacked even the simplest of genetic information, Darwin's guesses have dominated modern scientific thought like no other. Even his strongest proponents have admitted there have been significant problems with his theories and have merely offered Band-Aid guesses of their own. What Bertrand Russell once said may readily apply: 'The fact that an opinion is widely held is no evidence whatsoever that it is not utterly absurd.'"

Geoffrey Simmons, M.D., *What Darwin Didn't Know*, p. 41

In this booklet I will attempt to present and summarize information that is well-documented, observable, and makes common sense.

Macroevolution vs. Microevolution

Macroevolution is the theory that a species of plant or animal life can evolve over time into another species, or from a common ancestor. According to *Understanding Evolution, a* website created by the University of California, Berkeley as a resource for educators:

"Macroevolution encompasses the grandest trends and transformations in evolution, such as the origin of mammals and the radiation of flowering plants. Macroevolutionary patterns are generally what we see when we look at the large-scale history of life."

The Berkeley website states further that:

"It is not necessarily easy to 'see' macroevolutionary history; there are no firsthand accounts to be read. Instead, we reconstruct the history of life using all available evidence: geology, fossils, and living organisms. Once we've figured out *what* evolutionary events have taken place, we try to figure out *how* they happened. Just as in microevolution, basic evolutionary mechanisms—mutation, migration, genetic drift and natural selection—can produce major evolutionary change if given enough time."

In other words, scientists look at fossils, rocks, living animals and plants, and guess that they might be related to one another. They then try to guess what might have happened to cause these living organisms to change.

Microevolution refers to the changes that take place within a species; we see examples of microevolution every day. Microevolution can best be described as a variation within a population over time. There may be variation in existing genes or the loss of existing genetic information.

According to the Berkeley website, "Microevolution happens on a small scale (within a single population), while macroevolution happens on a scale that transcends the boundaries of a single species. Despite their differences, evolution at both of these levels relies on the same, established mechanisms of evolutionary change: mutation." Textbooks frequently use examples of microevolution to teach macroevolution, for which there is no real evidence or fossil record.

Biophysicist Dr. Kirk Durston points out that the definition of macroevolution is surprisingly imprecise for a scientific discipline:

"Macroevolution can be defined as evolution above the species level, or evolution on a 'grand scale,' or microevolution + 3.8 billion years. It has never been observed, but a theoretical example is the evolution from a chordate eel-like creature to a human being. Many people who embrace Darwinian evolution confidently state that evolution is a proven fact. They say this on the basis of thousands of papers discussing microevolution. Herein lies the second mistake . . . the assumption that because variation/microevolution is such an overwhelmingly proven fact that, therefore, macroevolution must be as well."

Kirk Durston, PhD, "Microevolution Versus Macroevolution: Two Mistakes," *Evolution News and Science Today*, July 16, 2015, https://evolutionnews.org

"When good teachers are teaching more advanced problems in mathematics, or in other subjects, they love a student who will argue that the textbook answer isn't correct. The reason isn't so much that the textbook answer might be wrong, although that always is a possibility. The real reason is that people learn the truth best if they fully understand the objections to the truth. If I believe in evolution (or anything else) only

because 'Teacher says so,' you could say I don't really believe in evolution. What I believe in is obedience to authority, and in letting 'Teacher' do my thinking for me. A democratic education aims to produce citizens who can think for themselves. Carl Sagan would have agreed emphatically, and he would have said that unquestioning acceptance of the dictates of authority is the opposite of the kind of skeptical thinking that science education ought to try to foster—except, of course, when it comes to evolutionary naturalism."
Phillip E. Johnson, *Defeating Darwinism,* pp. 48-49

Wolfgang Smith, PhD, mathematics; MIT professor and physicist has written:
"We are told dogmatically that [macro] evolution is an established fact; but we are never told who has established it, and by what means. We are told, often enough, that the doctrine is founded upon evidence, and that indeed this evidence is henceforward above all verification, as well as being immune from any subsequent contradiction by experience; but we are left entirely in the dark on the crucial question wherein, precisely, this evidence consists."
Smith, Wolfgang, PhD, *Teilhardism and the New*

Religion: A Thorough Analysis of the Teachings of de Chardin, 1988, pp. 1-2

When Charles Darwin visited the Galapagos Islands, he noted that turtles from the various islands could be recognized by minor differences in appearance. He also noted that finches varied by island—he was able to identify 13 different varieties of finches, classifying them by beak shape, color, and the types of food they ate. From those observations, Darwin surmised that the reasons for the variations could be attributed to chance mutations. Unfamiliar with the complexities of genetics, he reasoned that if the changes were inherited and helpful to the species, perhaps to help it survive in its environment, then through natural selection the changes would survive in the population. Darwin later theorized that with successive small visible changes within a population, perhaps over a long time one species could morph into a completely different species.

Jonathan Wells, PhD, professor of molecular and cell biology at Berkeley, explains in his abstract entitled "Homology in Biology" that although there are similarities between diverse creatures, e.g., bats, birds and butterflies all have wings, "this does not presuppose that they have derived from a common ancestor."

Dr. Wells then made the following observation: "[T]he eye of a mouse is structurally similar to the eye of an octopus, yet their supposed common ancestor did not possess such an eye. . . In 1859, Charles Darwin offered a different explanation for homology. According to Darwin, bats and whales possess similar bone structures because they inherited them from a common ancestor, not because they were constructed according to the same archetype. By replacing archetypes (which implied design and supernatural agency) with a natural mechanism such as common descent, Darwin hoped to render idealistic explanations unnecessary and to place biology on a securely naturalistic basis."

Jonathan Wells, "Homology in Biology, a Problem for Naturalistic Science," *The True Origin* Archive, April 21, 2020, https://trueorigin.org/homology.php

An alternative to the idea of common ancestry is the idea that the similarities between plants and animals might be present because they share the same Designer.

I remember learning about RNA and DNA back in high school. Most of us read a book called *The Double Helix* by biologists James Watson and Francis Crick. Apparently, each living being has a unique sequence—like a fingerprint. We all learned many years ago that RNA (the messenger) bonded with the DNA, giving the cells a blueprint of sorts for duplicating the DNA—certain amino acids, guanine (G), cytosine (C), adenine (A) and thymine (T) would only bond with certain other amino acids. Those four chemicals are combined in a unique way in each living organism; RNA, which transfers the DNA code, uses uracil (U), which is an unmethylated form of thymine.

Amusingly, scientists have discovered that we humans share approximately 60% of our DNA with a banana! To think of this in another way, perhaps, contrary to evolutionary thought, we do not share a common ancestor with a banana—perhaps our Designer simply used similar materials to create everything.

Anne Wojcicki, co-founder of 23 and Me, wrote the following that was printed in the New York Times:

"Even with three billion letter combinations in nearly every one of our cells, there is just a 0.5 percent difference between my DNA and the DNA of any other person on the planet. And the larger variations that do exist in genetic coding are responsible for the diversity of the world's species. While a banana, a mouse and a chimp look quite different from each other, as well as from you and me, their biological foundation and ours is still built from those four chemical letters: A, G, C and T. In fact, humans share about 60 percent of their DNA with a banana, 80 percent with a mouse and 96 percent with a chimp. A few simple switches in lettering and your AGCTs could have been the AGCTs of your neighbor or those of a banana."

Anne Wojcicki, "The Codes that Bind Us, and Set Us Apart," *The New York Times*, August 21, 2018, https://www.nytimes.com/2018/08/21/opinion/genetic-roots-of-humans.html

"When Watson and Crick discovered the helical structure of the DNA molecule and the general way that it coded the formation and replication of proteins in cells, there were great expectations that a plausible scientific explanation for the origin of life was just over the horizon. The laboratory synthesis of amino acids from basic chemicals further heightened the expectations that man, with all his intelligence and resources, could synthesize the living cell. These hopes have also been dashed with the failure to generate life in the laboratory, and researchers are stating that new natural laws will need to be discovered to explain how the high degree of order and specificity of even a single cell could be generated by random, natural processes." Luther D. Sunderland, *Darwin's Enigma*, p. 8

We have been taught that microevolution is a process that happens gradually through genetic mutations and natural selection. But consider, for example, the poodle and the golden retriever that are the same species as the wolf, yet have been bred for various traits. The variations among the dog breeds are not due to mutations, but rather, virtually all of the genetic possibilities were already present within the wolf—the breeders selected offspring with the desired traits, and within generations a new breed was formed. Certain traits were chosen and others eliminated.

If we were to simply look at the skeletons of the various dog breeds, the animals might appear to be completely unrelated—who would guess that the Chihuahua is of the same species as a St. Bernard? Nevertheless, dogs, wolves, coyotes, and dingoes are still canines, and as part of the same species, are able to mate with one another. The big cats, tigers and lions, leopards, and jaguars on occasion will cross breed, buffalo and cattle can mix, camels and llamas, various types of bears and even African and Indian elephants can have offspring. This demonstrates that much diversity is simply due to genetic variation within a species and illustrates the fact that change can take place within isolated populations. At one time there must have been one type of bear or big cat; most canines can be traced back to the wolf. Nevertheless, there is nothing in the fossil record which would point to one species becoming another species—there are genetic limits to change.

As with dog breeds, changes within a species can happen quite rapidly. A detailed explanation for this can be found in *The Natural Limits to Biological Change* by Lane Lester and Raymond Bohlin. In a nutshell, the authors maintain that there is a defined limit to the possible traits within each species, and that the environment can trigger genetic machinery

already present. As stated in chapter four, "not all biological change is dependent on new mutations . . . there already exists a great storehouse of genetic variation in natural populations. By simply reshuffling this variation, principally through recombination and migration, quite dramatic changes result."
Lane P. Lester, PhD & Raymond G. Bohlin, *The Natural Limits to Biological Change,* p. 69

According to Dr. Walt Brown, director of the Center for Scientific Creation:

"An offspring of a plant or animal has characteristics that vary commonly, often in subtle ways, from those of its parents. Because of the environment, genetics, and chance circumstances, some of these offspring will reproduce more than others. So, a species with certain characteristics will tend, on average, to have more children. In this sense, nature selects genetic characteristics suited to an environment—and, more importantly, eliminates unsuitable genetic variations. Therefore, an organism's gene pool is constantly decreasing. This is called natural selection. Notice, natural selection cannot produce new genes; it selects only among preexisting characteristics . . . variations are reduced, not increased."

Dr. Brown cites the experiments with Mendel's fruit flies. Different combinations are formed—not different genes. Mendel's laws show that there are limits to variation.

"Variations within organisms appear to be bounded."
Walt Brown, PhD, *In the Beginning, 8th Edition*, p. 7

Microevolution and People

Using human reproduction as an example, Lester and Bohlin explain in *The Natural Limits to Biological Change* that meiosis [the division of cells in the process of reproduction] could result in great variation even between siblings: each person receives a set of 23 chromosomes from each parent.

"Since each pair can split one of two ways, there are 2 to the 23rd possible gametes or 8,388 times 8,388, which means that each couple could produce children with 70 trillion possible differences."
Lane P. Lester, PhD & Raymond G. Bohlin, *The Natural Limits to Biological Change*, p. 54

"Microevolution is without controversy and was known about and recognized long before Darwin came along. It has long been accepted that plants, animals and humans may experience minor changes or 'adaptations' in response to variances in the environment—such as lighter skin in colder climates, which enhances vitamin D production—as opposed to warmer climates where darker skin protects against excess sun damage. But these types of

adaptations do not change one species into another. In scientific terms, small changes—microevolution—do not cause major changes as in turning a monkey or some purported ape-like ancestor into a human."
Sharon Sebastian & Raymond G. Bohlin, PhD, *Darwin's Racists*, pp. 137-138

The body can manufacture vitamin D3, needed for a variety of reasons, including strong bones and a healthy immune system, from direct sunlight. Those who live far from the Equator would develop a light skin color to help them absorb more sunlight; those who live near the Equator would develop a darker skin to absorb less sunlight—in each case, those genes would be passed on to their children. An exception might be Eskimos (Inuits), who have darker skin, yet live in Arctic latitudes. However, their traditional diet includes fish-liver oils containing large amounts of vitamin D_3.

A population of people, or any other form of life, has many genetic possibilities. If a few members of a population move to an isolated region, such as an island, the new group will have a different and smaller set of genetic characteristics (or a smaller range of genetic potential) than the entire population. As a result, later generations on that island will have traits that differ from the original population. Natural selection filters out certain parental genes in successive generations, producing offspring with slightly different characteristics but less genetic variability.

According to Nina G. Jablonski and George Chaplin, in their research article "Human Skin Pigmentation as an Adaptation to UV Radiation," published in the journal *Proceedings of the National Academy of Scientists*:

"As hominins dispersed outside of the tropics, they experienced different intensities and seasonal mixtures of UVA and UVB. Extreme UVA throughout the year and two equinoctial peaks of UVB prevail within the tropics. Under these conditions, the primary selective pressure was to protect folate by maintaining dark pigmentation. Photolysis of folate and its main serum form of 5-methylhydrofolate is caused by UVR and by reactive oxygen species generated by UVA. Competition for folate between the needs for cell division, DNA repair, and melanogenesis is severe under stressful, high-UVR conditions and is exacerbated by dietary insufficiency."

Nina G. Jablonski, PhD and George Chaplin, PhD, "Human Skin Pigmentation as an Adaptation to UV Radiation," *Proceedings of the National Academy of Scientists,* May 11, 2010, p. 107, https://www.pnas.org/content/107/Supplement_2/8962

Mitochondrial Eve / Y Chromosome Male

In human cells, the nucleus contains all the cell's genetic material, an equal amount from each parent, with the exception of what is called mitochondrial DNA (mtDNA). The mitochondria are organelles that exist outside the nucleus in the cytoplasm of each cell, and their function is to convert energy from food into a form which can be used by the cells. During reproduction, recombination does not occur in the mtDNA—it is a small strand which is passed on only from the mother, and with the exception of a rare mutation, it does not change from generation to generation. A 1987 study at Berkeley led by geneticists Rebecca Cann, PhD, Mark Stoneking, PhD, and Charles Wilson, PhD, compared the mitochondrial DNA from people across the globe, and they were found to have had the same female ancestor, now referred to by scientists as "Mitochondrial Eve."

"In 'Mitochondrial DNA and Human Evolution,' Cann, Stoneking, and Wilson reported their analysis of mtDNA from 147 people from five different geographic regions including Africa, Asia, Australia (aboriginal), Europe, and New Guinea (aboriginal). The authors investigated how, when, and where the human gene pool

arose and migrated. . . [The] article postulated that the African woman was probably a member of a small population of modern *Homo sapiens* living in Africa. Cann, Stoneking, and Wilson said that she was the only woman whose mtDNA survived until 1987."
Dorothy L. Haskett, "Mitochondrial DNA and Human Evolution," *The Embryo Project Encyclopedia*, October 10, 2014, https://embryo.asu.edu/pages/mitochondrial-dna-and-human-evolution-1987-rebecca-louise-cann-mark-stoneking-and-allan

While the above study postulated that the "Mitochondrial Eve" lived approximately 200,000 years ago, scientists have conducted studies on the rate of mutations which occur in the mitochondrial DNA, and have shortened that time frame to less than 6,500 years ago, creating some dissonance among evolutionary scientists.

"Regardless of the cause, evolutionists are most concerned about the effect of a faster mutation rate. For example, researchers have calculated [previously] that 'Mitochondrial Eve—the woman whose mtDNA was ancestral to that in all living people—lived 100,000 to 200,000 years ago in Africa. Using the new clock, she would be a mere 6,000 years old."

Ann Gibbons, "Calibrating the Mitochondrial Clock,"
Science, January 2, 1998, Vol. 279, p. 29,
http://www.dnai.org/teacherguide/pdf/reference_r
omanovs.pdf

A 1997 study based on frequency of mutations
which occur in mtDNA, conducted by geneticist
Lawrence Loewe, PhD, of the School of
Biological Sciences, University of Edinburgh,
Scotland, and Professor Siegfried Sherer, PhD,
of the Microbiology Department at the
Technical University of Munich, concluded: "If
molecular evolution is really neutral at these
sites [occurs at a constant rate at all sites],
such a high mutation rate would indicate that
Eve lived about 6,500 years ago—a figure
clearly incompatible with current theories on
human origins."
Lawrence Lowe, PhD, "Mitochondrial Eve: The Plot
Thickens," *Trends in Ecology & Evolution*, Vol. 12,
November 11, 1997, p. 422

A similar study was published in 1997 by
biochemist Thomas J. Parsons, PhD of the
University of Washington. As a postdoctoral
fellow at the Smithsonian Institution in
Washington, D.C., and during a research
faculty appointment at the University of
Nebraska, Dr. Parsons focused on ancient

DNA, molecular evolution and population genetics. He concluded:

"Thus, our observation of the substitution rate, 2.5/site/Myr [million years], is roughly 20-fold higher than would be predicted from phylogenetic analyses [evolution studies]. Using our empirical rate to calibrate the mtDNA molecular clock would result in an average age of the mtDNA MRCA [most recent common ancestor] of only ~6,500 y.a. [years ago], clearly incompatible with the known age of modern humans."
Thomas J. Parsons, PhD, et al., "A High Observed Substitution Rate in the Human Mitochondrial DNA Control Region," *Nature Genetics*, April 1997, Vol. 15, p. 365,
https://www.nature.com/articles/ng0497-363

According to discoveries made by genetic research scientists, there is virtually no change in the Y chromosome that is passed from fathers to sons. Females have two X chromosomes, whereas males have one X and one Y. Unlike what occurs with the other 22 non-sex chromosomes, there is no swapping of DNA during reproduction, and the Y chromosome is passed intact. An occasional alteration can occur in the DNA of the chromosome, causing a slight change in the genetic sequence, thereby, male family history can be traced through the Y chromosome.

Peter Underhill, PhD, senior research scientist in the Department of Genetics at Stanford University, and Peter Oefner, PhD, biochemist and associate director of the Stanford Genome Technology Center, have found that all men have a common ancestor who originated in Africa. By examining small differences in the DNA of the male Y chromosome, they have been able to trace the migration of world populations.

"The two scientists have now found 160 DNA substitutions on the Y chromosome. They have catalogued these changes in 1062 men from 21 populations and have concluded that a small group of East Africans (Sudanese and Ethiopians) and Khoisan, from Southern Africa, are the closest present-day relatives of the original ancestral male lineage. The genetic data also revealed that there were at least two migrations of modern humans into the Americas. People in the first migration traveled to the Americas from Africa via East Asia. The second wave of immigrants traveled from Africa through Central Asia into North America. According to the researchers, the predominant Y chromosomes in Native American populations today are most closely related to individuals in Central Asia."

Weidenbach, Kristin, "Why Study the Y: Chromosome Reveals Path of Ancestral Humans," *Stanford Report*, November 8, 2000, https://news.stanford.edu/news/2000/november8/chromosome-1108.html

According to research conducted by Dr. Nathaniel Jeanson, who earned his PhD in cell and developmental biology from Harvard University:

"We found that the mutation rates from the high coverage studies explained the branch lengths of the Y chromosome tree within just a few thousand years (fig. 1). We also found that these rates rejected the evolutionary time of origin for the first modern *Homo sapiens* (fig. 2). For simplicity, when measuring total branch lengths, we began by simply adopting the typical evolutionary root position. Conversely, based on the results of the accompanying paper (Jeanson 2019), we also explored an alternative, better-supported (see Jeanson 2019) root position, and we found that the high coverage Y chromosome mutation rate explained all but the most divergent haplogroup A branch lengths in about 4,500 years."

Nathaniel T. Jeanson, PhD, and Ashley D. Holland,

"Evidence for a Human Y Chromosome Molecular Clock: Pedigree-Based Mutation Rates Suggest a 4,500-Year History for Human Paternal Inheritance," *Answers Research Journal,* December 4, 2019, https://answersingenesis.org/theory-of-evolution/molecular-clock/evidence-human-y-chromosome-molecular-clock/

Missing Links

The story of the supposed missing links between man and ape is built upon fraud and fantasy. Clearly, scientists did not see evidence and develop a theory—the theory was in place, and there has been a desire to find evidence to support that theory. However, the theory is not supported by the fossil record. Even evolutionary scientists, who believe in a very old earth, can point to a time called the Cambrian Explosion when most of the major groups of animals first appeared in the fossil record. Interestingly, there are no fossils that can substantiate evolutionary claims of common ancestry or one species morphing into another, let alone links between man and ape, as Darwin supposed. Missing links between species are truly missing. That idea is unproven and depends on sensationalism and the imagination of artists to lend credibility.

Very telling are the full titles of Darwin's books: *On the Origin of Species by Means of Natural Selection, or the Preservation of Favoured Races in the Struggle for Life,* and its sequel, *The Descent of Man,* in which he theorized that man evolved from apes or from a common ancestor, and that some races became more developed than others. Sadly, in the name of science, people have used Darwin's theories to justify their own racist tendencies, including slavery, oppression, extermination, and the eugenics movement. Perhaps scientists grasp these theories as an alternatetive to a belief in Divine creation.

"For over a century skulls and teeth have produced unreliable conclusions about man's origin. Also, fossil evidence allegedly supporting human evolution is fragmentary and open to other interpretations. Fossil evidence showing the evolution of chimpanzees, supposedly the closest living relative to humans, is nonexistent."
Walt Brown, PhD, *In the Beginning, 8th Edition,* 2008, p. 13

Dr. Henry Gee, senior editor of Biological Sciences at *Nature* magazine, wrote the following:

"We have all seen the canonical parade of apes, each one becoming more human. We know that as a depiction of evolution, this line-up is tosh [tidy, but sheer nonsense]. Yet we cling to it. Ideas of what human evolution ought to have been like still colour our debates ...

almost every time someone claims to have found a new species of hominin, someone else refutes it. The species is said to be either a member of Homo sapiens, but pathological, or an ape."
Henry Gee, PhD, Biochemist, "Paleoanthropology: Craniums with Clout," *Nature*, October 5, 2011, https://www.nature.com/articles/478034a

"How is it that trained men, the greatest experts of their day, could look at a set of modern human bones—the cranial fragments—and 'see' a clear simian signature in them; and 'see' in an ape's jaw the unmistakable signs of humanity? The answers, inevitably, have to do with the scientists' expectations and their effects on the interpretation of data."
Roger Lewin, PhD, Biochemist, *Bones of Contention*, p. 61

"Nothing excites our interest more than that which offers some hint concerning the origin of our own species. More than one obscure paleontologist has become famous overnight by announcing sensational and extravagant claims following the find of some fragmentary remains of a creature he believes to be related to man's origin, especially if the find was made in some

remote area of Africa or Asia. As we shall see, most such claims eventually fade into obscurity as further research and discoveries invalidate the claims, and in a few cases sensational 'finds' have been exposed as hoaxes."
Duayne T.Gish, PhD, *Evolution: The Fossils Still Say No!*, p. 226

I remember drawings of embryos from my high school biology textbook, showing the similarities between the embryos of animals from that of a chicken to that of a human being. I didn't know that those drawings were falsified, and hopefully, neither did the publisher of the textbooks! Heckel admitted to having embellished the drawings to overstate any similarities. Neverthless, these drawings and close replicas are still found in textbooks which have been printed as recently as 2011.

The following are several examples of supposed "missing links" between man and apes. What seems amazing to me is that in the enthusiasm to find those "missing links," incredible liberties have been taken from fragmental skeletal remains; in fact, as we see with the Nebraska Man, the tooth of a pig gave rise to sensational depictions of an ape-man swinging a club. The Java Man was discovered to have been a hoax, composed of human and orangutan bones; the Piltdown Man was a fraud, composed of a baboon jaw and chimpanzee teeth, filed and stained to resemble those of humans; and all that the discoverers of the Ramapithecus had were a few teeth and jaw fragments, which were later shown to have been incorrectly pieced together. Yet "illustrations" of ape men have been studied in textbooks for years! The famous "Lucy" the Australopithecine, is composed of 47 bone fragments that were found out of a supposed 207 bones, dubiously held together by plaster of Paris. Not only are these specimens still referenced in textbooks, but some still appear in museums and on the web pages of respected scientific publications.

Nebraska Man (Hesperopithecus)

Upon the discovery of a tooth in a farmer's field, the Nebraska Man, a supposed "missing link" between man and ape, caught the excitement of evolutionists all over the world. The story helped to shape the sentiment and outcome surrounding the 1925 Scopes Monkey Trial, paving the way for evolutionists to teach evolution in public schools. Interestingly, a decade later, it was discovered that the tooth fit well into the jaw of an extinct hog. The following illustration appeared in the London News in 1922:

"In 1917 a farmer and part time geologist named Harold Cook who lived in Nebraska found a single tooth that looked similar to an ape or human molar. About five years later, he sent it to be examined by Henry Osborn at Columbia University. Osborn excitedly declared this fossil to be a tooth from the first ever discovered ape-like man in North America. The single tooth grew in popularity and throughout the world and it wasn't long before a drawing of the Nebraska Man showed up in a London periodical."
Heather Scoville, Biochemist, "Nebraska Man—An Evolution Hoax," *ThoughtCo*, January 27, 2020, https://www.thoughtco.com/nebraska-man-1224737

In 1927 more fossils were discovered in that same area, and it was finally deduced that the tooth fit the skull of an extinct hog.

The National Center for Science Education published a journal called *Creation/Evolution Journal* from 1980 to 1997. It was originally published by the American Humanist Association, and it was acquired by NCSE in 1991. Its stated purpose was to support the teaching of evolution and to respond to arguments used by creationists. The following article appeared in the journal in 1985:

"In 1922, solely on the basis of a worn fossil tooth from Nebraska, paleontologist Henry Fairfield Osborn described *Hesperopithecus haroldcookii* as the first anthropoid ape from North America. Five years later, Osborn's colleague William King Gregory concluded that the tooth most likely came from an extinct peccary, a pig-like animal. During its brief life, *Hesperopithecus* provoked intemperate speculations about its relation to humans, including a 'reconstruction' of 'Nebraska Man' by an artist in a popular British tabloid news magazine. The Nebraska tooth also sparked some memorable exchanges between Osborn and William Jennings Bryan, from whose home state the tooth had come. Osborn apparently began to have doubts about his identification of the tooth shortly before the Scopes 'monkey trial' in July 1925, and he stopped mentioning it in his publications."

John Wolf and James Mellett, "The Role of the Nebraska Man in the Creation/Evolution Debate," *Creation/Evolution Journal*, Summer 1985, Vol. 5, No.2, https://ncse.ngo/role-nebraska-man-creation-evolution-debate

Paleontologist Brian Switeg, science author for *National Geographic*, wrote that even as a student of evolutionary biology at Rutgers University, he had been able to discern that a pig's tooth in the science lab had not come from a human being. As a science blogger, he wrote the following:

"Much to the embarrassment of Osborn and other researchers that had studied and defended *Hesperopithecus*, the tooth turned out to be from a peccary rather than any primate, and this cautionary paleoanthropological tale is celebrated amongst creationists as they feel it proves the dishonesty and feeble-mindedness of evolutionary researchers as a whole. As with any other piece of evidence a creationist may marshal, however, the story of the "discovery" of *Hesperopithecus* is a complex mesh of political, social, and institutional factors that ended up creating a man from a molar."
Brian Switeg, *"The Truth About the Nebraska Man,"* *Science Blogs*, February 21, 2008, https://scienceblogs.com/laelaps/2008/02/21/the-truth-about-nebraska-man

Java Man (Homo Erectus)

In 1892 Eugene Dubois found a thigh bone, which appeared to be human, on the island of Java. In 1893 he found a large skull cap, and later three teeth close to the same site. Dubois thought he had found the "missing link," and proof of human evolution—he renamed it Pithecanthropus erectus. Other scientists have since identified two of the teeth as belonging to an orangutan. Some 30 years later, Dubois admitted that he had found two human skulls at the same location. Nonetheless, one can find the Java Man in science textbooks.

"In 1892 a Dutch physician, Eugene Dubois, set sail to the Dutch East Indies (now called Indonesia). Completely enamored by the theory

of evolution, he had come to believe for some reason that he would find the elusive 'missing link' between humans and apes in that part of the world. On the island of Java, he found a thigh-bone, which to all intents and purposes was like that of modern humans. About a year earlier in the same location he had found a large skull-cap, and later three teeth. These were not necessarily from the same individual: the skullcap and the leg-bone were about 15 meters (50 feet) apart . . . There is no reason to insist that the skullcap and the leg bone came from the same individual. But Dubois had found his 'missing link' and it eventually became widely accepted as such, in spite of the fact that a leading authority had identified two of the teeth as those of an orangutan, and the other as human. 'Java Man' was trumpeted around the world as indisputable proof of human evolution. Textbooks and magazines were filled with fanciful reconstructing of 'Java Man', who had been given the impressive-sounding scientific name of *Pithecanthropus erectus* ('erect ape-man'). Naturally, the bones did not show whether their owner (or owners) had much body hair or not. Yet drawings of 'Java Man' all showed the required amount of hair, the usual club in the hand, and so on. Although no face bones had been found, suitably 'half-ape, half-man' features were reconstructed in

artists' drawings."
Carl Wieland, "Who Was Java Man?," *Creation Ministries International*, June 1991, pp. 22-23, https://creation.com/who-was-java-man

Piltdown Man (Eoanthropus Dawsonii)

Amateur archaeologist Charles Dawson supposedly discovered the Piltdown Man in 1912. Composed of an ape's jaw and a human skull, it turned out to be a fraud. Dawson claimed that a workman at the Piltdown gravel pit had discovered the skull and had broken it up in the belief that it was a coconut fossil. Dawson found further fragments of the skull and took them to Arthur Woodward, paleontologist with the British Museum. Woodward opined that the Piltdown Man was a missing link between apes and people. It was not until 1953 that it was proven to be a forgery—chimpanzee teeth had been stained and filed and fitted into the lower jaw of an orangutan to appear more human.

"Upon closer examination of the Piltdown Man, scientists found that the presumed hominid's skull and jaw actually originated from two different species, a human and an ape (possibly an orangutan). A microscope revealed that the teeth within the jaw had been filed down to make them look more human, and that many of the remains from the Piltdown site appeared to have been stained to match each other as well as the gravel where they were supposedly found. In November 1953, authorities of the British Natural History Museum announced these findings and publicly called Piltdown Man a fraud."

Pruitt, Sarah, "Piltdown Man Hoax," *History*, December 18, 2012, https://www.history.com/news/piltdown-man-hoax-100-years-ago

"Since 1953, it has been universally acknowledged that Piltdown 'Man' was a hoax, yet Piltdown 'Man' was in textbooks for more than 40 years."

Walt Brown, PhD, *In the Beginning, 8th Edition*, p.13

"In 1912, Charles Dawson, an amateur archaeologist in England, claimed he'd made one of the most important fossil discoveries ever. Ultimately, however, his 'Piltdown Man' proved to be a hoax. By cleverly pairing a human skull with an orangutan's jaw-stained to match and give the appearance of age–a mysterious forger duped the scientific world. In the decades between the find's unearthing and the revelation it was fraudulent, people in the United States and around the world learned about Piltdown Man as a 'missing link' connecting ape and man. Newspaper articles, scientific publications and museum exhibitions all presented Piltdown Man as a legitimate scientific discovery supporting a particular vision of human evolution."

Samuel Redman, PhD, "What the Piltdown Man Hoax from 1912 Can Teach Science Today," *The Conversation,* U Mass Amherst, May 4, 2017, https://theconversation.com/behind-closed-doors-what-the-piltdown-man-hoax-from-1912-can-teach-science-today-76967

Proconsul Ramapithecus

The Ramapithecus is still referred to in some textbooks and encyclopedias as an important link in human evolution. The only evidence for it consisted of a few teeth and jaw fragments, which when assembled looked almost human-like. Eventually the opposing jaw was found with some facial bones attached, which showed that the previous reconstructions had been incorrect. The supposed "missing link" appears to have been an orangutan.

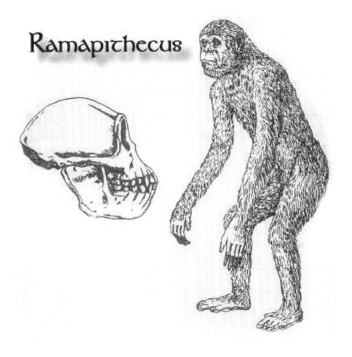

Ramapithecus

"Some textbooks still claim that Ramapithecus is man's ancestor, an intermediate between man and some ape-like ancestor. This mistaken belief resulted from piecing together, in 1932, fragments of upper teeth and bones into the two large pieces . . . This was done so the shape of the jaw resembled the parabolic arch of man. . . . In 1977, a complete lower jaw of Ramapithecus was found. The true shape of the jaw was not parabolic, but rather U-shaped, distinctive of apes."
Walt Brown, PhD, *In the Beginning, , 8th Edition,* 2008, p. 13

"It is no slight matter that Ramapithecus was in the books as our Miocene ancestor for fifteen years before the Tooth Fairy struck on the rebound and transformed him back into a quaint old ape. The respected professionals wrote, as many did, that 'there is general agreement' on the relevance of Ramapithecus to man's origin, it naturally affects the opinions of other professionals and of the general public, contributing to the sentiment that human evolution is a proven fact with only certain stages and details to be filled in. As with the Hesperopithecus [Nebraska Man], anthropologists were not victims of fake fossils as they were in the Piltdown case; they were victims of their own imaginations, their willingness to extrapolate sensational conclusions from minimal data and to publish these in the name of science."

William R. Fix, *Bone Peddlers*, 1984, p. 23

Australopithecus (Lucy)

What is interesting to me is that museums have very differing displays related to Lucy. Only 47 bone fragments were found out of a supposed 207 bones, and the rest of Lucy is composed of plaster of Paris and imagination. If a museum has an evolutionary story to tell, Lucy may appear to have shorter arms and more human-like features. Creationist museums depict her as an ape.

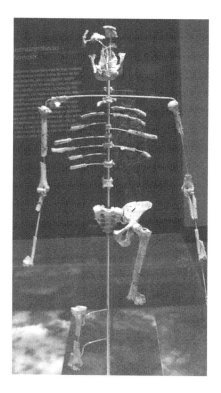

According to the Institution for Creation Research Discovery Center, "Not only do these bone pieces have no dates on them, but no one can be absolutely sure they are even from the same individual. The pieces fit where the biased researcher would like them to go. Whatever fragments are missing must be filled in with plaster of Paris and imagination. This is certainly true with Lucy. Her bones are what would be expected on the basis of creation: "Lucy's fossil remains match up remarkably well with the bones of a pygmy chimp."

Frank Sherwin, "Lucy Languishes as a Human-Ape Link," *Institute for Creation Research*, April 28, 2017, https://www.icr.org/article/lucy-languishes-human-ape-link/

"Unfortunately, there is very little fossil evidence to go on. Even though Lucy is fairly complete for a mammal fossil (47 of 207 bones found), the bones are mostly small fragments with many pieces missing. Other specimens have been found, but they are far more fragmentary. No matter how complete, all fossils must be interpreted. Some interpretation is always left to the imagination of the person doing the reconstruction. . . Lucy's bones are not only broken but also missing many key features. For example, there is very little to go on to

reconstruct her skull. It is completely shattered. All of her upper face is missing. So is the foramen magnum, the place where the skull attaches to the spine. Other specimens have been found with this part of the skull largely complete, but even they have to be reconstructed from fragments, which leave large gaps, allowing for several interpretations. Some evolutionists give her a small braincase, while others a large braincase. Most place the skull on the spine at a point where human skulls rest. However, those same pieces can be fitted together to depict a more ape-like skull. . . It is important to understand that Lucy's broken leg bones would actually fit together just fine with short, ape-like proportions."
Doug Henderson, "Bringing Lucy to Life," *Answers Magazine,* January 1, 2013, https://answersingenesis.org/human-evolution/lucy/bringing-lucy-to-life/

"At present we have no grounds for thinking that there was anything distinctively human about australopithecine ecology and behavior . . . [T]hey were surprisingly ape-like in skull form, premolar dentition, limb proportions, and morphology of some joint surfaces, and they may still have been spending a significant amount of time in the trees."

Matt Cartmill, PhD, et al., "One Hundred Years of Paleoanthropology," *American Scientist*, July– August 1986, Vol. 74, p. 417, https://www.jstor.org/stable/i27854244

"Evolutionary scientists consider this fossil discovery to be significant because it demonstrates that diverse species of early human ancestors coexisted in time and space. However, while there may well have once been multiple species of australopithecine apes in Africa, australopithecine fossils are the remains of extinct apes and have no connection to humanity's lineage. They were animals. The dates assigned to Lucy and other fossils from the region, as we have discussed elsewhere, are vastly inflated products of unverifiable worldview-based interpretations. Australopithecine apes, whether in South Africa or East Africa were not stepping-stones on the road to becoming human."

Mitchell, Elizabeth, PhD, "What Can Lucy's Neighbors Tell Us About Human Origins?," *Answers in Genesis*, February 25, 2019, https://answersingenesis.org/human-evolution/ape-man/what-can-lucys-neighbors-tell-us-about-human-origins/

Neanderthal Man

The Neanderthal Man was depicted for years as a primitive caveman, an indisputable missing link. I have to laugh because my nephew, a physician, had his DNA tested and was horrified to discover he was about 2% Neanderthal. Truth be told, most people of European or Asian descent have some Neanderthal heritage. Scientists make much of the fact that this people group no longer exists. However, if we consider the history of Native Americans, we can understand that many of us carry them with us as part of our genetic heritage, although due to diseases and conflicts with European settlers, some tribes no longer exist. The truth is that the Neanderthal was intelligent and fully human.

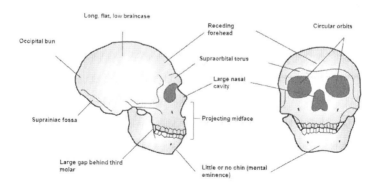

"For about 100 years, the world was led to believe that Neanderthal Man was stooped and ape-like. This false idea was based upon some Neanderthals with bone diseases, such as arthritis and rickets. Recent dental and x-ray studies of Neanderthals suggest that they were humans who matured at a slower rate and lived to be much older than people today. Neanderthal Man, Heidelberg Man, and Cro-Magnon Man are now considered completely human. Artists' drawings of "ape-men," especially their fleshy portions, are often quite imaginative and are not supported by the evidence."

Walt Brown PhD, *In the Beginning, 8th Edition,* p. 14

"Neanderthals, traditionally designated Homo sapiens, were not only 'human' but also, it turns out, more 'modern' than scientists previously allowed. 'In the minds of European anthropologists who first studied them, Neanderthals were the embodiment of primitive humans, sub humans if you will,' says Fred H. Smith, a physical anthropologist at Loyola University in Chicago, who has been studying Neanderthal DNA. 'They were believed to be scavengers who made primitive tools and were

incapable of language or symbolic thought.'
Now, he says, researchers believe that
Neanderthals 'were highly intelligent, able to
adapt to a wide variety of ecological zones, and
capable of developing highly functional tools to
help them do so. They were quite
accomplished."

Joe Alper, "Rethinking Neanderthals," *Smithsonian Magazine*, June 2003, Vol. 34, Iss. 3, p. 82, https://www.smithsonianmag.com/science-nature/rethinking-neanderthals-83341003/

"Everyone living outside of Africa today has a
small amount of Neanderthal in them, carried
as a living relic of these ancient encounters. A
team of scientists comparing the full genomes
of the two species concluded that most
Europeans and Asians have approximately
2 percent Neanderthal DNA. Indigenous sub-
Saharan Africans have none, or very little
Neanderthal DNA because their ancestors did
not migrate through Eurasia."

Geographic Project, "Why Am I Neanderthal?," *National Geographic*, https://genographic.nationalgeographic.com/neanderthal/

"Neanderthals are some of history's worst victims of bad PR. As we continue to discover, Neanderthals weren't crude, uncultured hominins but rather a complex species with sophisticated tools, engravings, and attitudes toward foreigners–albeit with a potential taste for inbreeding. A PNAS study clears up another misconception we Homo sapiens have always lorded over them: their terrible posture. . . Depictions of Neanderthals in pop culture usually show a large-browed hunched-over individual who looks more like a great ape on all fours than an upright human. That reputation stemmed from a single skeleton from an elderly Neanderthal discovered in La Chapelle-aux-Saints in France, described in 1911 by Marcellin Boule. But as new virtual reconstruction of the Neanderthal's skeleton reveals, he and his kin had the type of skeleton that could walk as perfectly upright as any good-postured human today."
Yasmin Tayag, "Neanderthals Weren't Hunched Over–They Walked Upright," *Inverse,* February 25, 2019, www.inverse.com/article/53560

"After the discovery of DNA, groups of scientists set about mapping the genome of modern humans to unravel the mysteries of humanity from deep within our genes. Yet another group embarked upon the ambitious project to map the genome of Neanderthals, taking bits of DNA from the bones of these ancient people. What they learned from this project was surprising: Perhaps the Neanderthals didn't all perish thousands of years ago. In the DNA of European Caucasians and some Asians, Neanderthal genes popped up."

Karen Harris, "Our Image of Neanderthals Is All Wrong: The First Skeleton Was Arthritic," *Ancient History*, August 20, 2019, https://historydaily.org/our-image-of-neanderthals-is-all-wrong-the-first-skeleton-was-arthritic/

Cro-Magnon Man

I remember attending a seminar years ago at which the speaker dressed a depiction of the Cro-Magnon Man in a suit and tie. It startled me because he resembled my late Uncle Ted! Note that in the excerpts below that some of the authors are still using evolutionary dates, however, there is really no dispute among evolutionists and creationists that the Cro-Magnon Man was fully human.

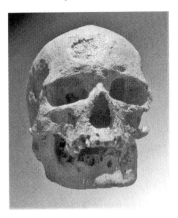

"Some 40,000 years ago, Cro-Magnons—the first people who had a skeleton that looked anatomically modern—entered Europe, coming from Africa. A [study by a] group of geneticists, coordinated by Guido Barbujani and David Caramelli of the Universities of Ferrara and Florence, shows that a Cro-Magnoid individual who lived in Southern Italy 28,000 years ago was a modern European, genetically as well as anatomically."

David Caramelli, PhD, et al, "Europe's Ancestors: Cro-Magnon 28,000 Years Old Had DNA Like Modern Humans," *Science Daily*, July 16, 2008, https://www.sciencedaily.com/releases/2008/07/0 80715204741.htm

"Cro-Magnons lived in rock shelters and hunted wooly mammoths, but that doesn't mean they were *becoming* human—they were fully human like us. These people were skilled artists and left exquisite carvings and paintings. Archaeologists haven't found any hint of crude scratches or splashes from some imagined pre-human. Cro-Magnons made jewelry from teeth, shells, and tusks. They painted and carved colorful pictures of their prey, sometimes with graphic mortal wounds, on apparently sacred cave walls. They used earth minerals, charcoal, and animal fat to craft their paints, which they carefully applied as liquids or powders."

Brian Thomas, PhD, "Who Were Cro-Magnon People?," *Acts and Facts*, November 30, 2017, https://www.icr.org/article/who-were-cro-magnon-people

"The new belief is that the physical dimensions of the so-called 'Cro-Magnon' are not sufficiently different enough from modern humans to warrant a separate designation." K. Kris Hirst, "Why Don't We Call Them Cro-Magnon Anymore?" *ThoughtCo.*, November 14, 2019, https://www.thoughtco.com/we-dont-call-them-cro-magnon-170738

March of Progress

I recall seeing a longer version of the sketch below on the back of cereal boxes when I was growing up. The sketch, called the March of Progress, appeared in Time-Life Books in 1965. The progression goes from a bent-over ape to man, walking upright. The full sketch contained 15 figures progressing from ape to man, reprinted and frequently hung on classroom walls. Note that the depictions of the apes are bipedal. Also note that in the full progression the final sketch is that of a light-skinned European male.

"Despite the lack of evidence, the Darwinian view of human origins was soon enshrined in drawings that showed a knuckle-walking ape evolving through a series of intermediate forms into an upright human being. Such drawings have subsequently appeared in countless textbooks, museum exhibits, magazine articles,

and even cartoons. They constitute the ultimate icon of evolution, because they symbolize the implications of Darwin's theory for the ultimate meaning of human existence."
Jonathan Wells, PhD, *Icons of Evolution*, 2002, p. 211

"No tool has been as successful in promoting human evolution as have been the pictures and reconstructions of our ancient ancestors. Since no one has ever seen these ancient ancestors, the abilities of the artists who constructed them have been nothing short of miraculous. It gives the term 'science fiction' a whole new meaning. . . From a scientific point of view, their drawings and reconstructions are outrageous."
Marvin L. Lubenow, *Bones of Contention*, Baker Publishing Company, 2004, p. 38

"As Lubenow summarizes, the parade 'is raw propaganda—brilliant propaganda, but raw nonetheless,' and few evolutionists have 'protested this gross lack of scientific objectivity' shown in the Time-Life and other books. Yet this outrageous and raw propaganda has no doubt influenced millions of persons to accept the Darwinian worldview of human evolution and is, by far, the most popular icon of evolution that has been presented everywhere in the media for decades."

Jerry Bergman, PhD, "The Ape-to-Human progression: The Most Common Evolution Icon is a Fraud," *Journal of Creation*, March 23, 2009, https://creation.com/images/pdfs/tj/j23_3/j23_3_1 6-20.pdf

Young Earth

Scientists use several dating methods to determine the age of the earth and its contents. Certain assumptions must be made beforehand, as one rock might be dated based on the supposed age of another rock or fossil. Young earth scientists have also questioned the fact that the evolutionary model makes no allowance for the rates of change of processes to have fluctuated over time. In other words, there is no neutral testing method—assumptions lead to conclusions, and any data which does not correspond to expectations may be tossed aside as a testing error. Note that most cultures have stories of a worldwide flood—layers of rocks and debris would have formed over a very short time and buried pre-existing forests, temporarily changing the atmosphere. Also note that the catastrophic worldwide flood was probably accompanied by volcanic action and monsoon type rains—rushing water would have carved out rock formations and vastly changed the face of our earth. Here is a simple experiment anyone can try at home: Fill a jar or test tube with water, sand, gravel, shells, etc., and then shake it up and watch the layers form.

"Perhaps the most widely used argument for a millions-of-years-old earth historically has been the rock layers of the geologic column. It would take millions of years for the thousands of meters of material beneath us to accumulate and lithify—or so the argument goes. Is that true? A polystrate fossil is a single fossil [of a single organism] that spans more than one geologic stratum. Many polystrate tree trunk fossils have been discovered, as well as a baleen whale, swamp plants called calamites, and catfish. Polystrate fossils prove that both the rock layers of the geologic column and the surfaces between them do not require millions of years of slow and gradual accumulation and lithification. After all, how could a tree escape its inevitable decay while sticking out of the ground for millions of years with its roots dead and lithified, while it waited to be slowly covered with sediment? Polystrate fossils provide evidence that the rock strata have formed rapidly—fast enough to preserve organic materials before their decay."

Jeff Miller, PhD, "21 Reasons to Believe the Earth is Young," *Apologetics Press*, http://apologeticspress.org/APContent.aspx?category=9&article=5641

Sedimentary rock by definition is rock which had been deposited by water. Also noteworthy is the fact that erosion between the rock layers is virtually nonexistent, which does not make sense if the rocks were formed over millions of years.

Carbon-14 is mostly used to date organic material. Plants take in both carbon-12 and carbon-14, which are found in the same ratios in the atmosphere—a ratio of about 1 to 1 trillion. When a living organism dies, it no longer takes in radiocarbon. Scientists have determined that carbon-14 has a half life of approximately 5,730 years, so therefore, after 60,000 years, there should be virtually no carbon-14 left in the fossil. Yet, using newer more sensitive equipment, young earth scientists have found radio carbon in materials such as coal, which old earth scientists have dated as millions of years old. Note that a catastrophic world flood would skew the ratio between carbon-12 and carbon-14 for a period of time, such that anything buried prior to the flood could appear to be older than it actually is. The following articles point to findings which are considered controversial by mainstream evolutionary science:

"Dr. Thomas Seiler, a physicist from Germany, gave the presentation in Singapore. He said that his team and the laboratories they employed took special care to avoid contamination. That included protecting the samples, avoiding cracked areas in the bones, and meticulous pre-cleaning of the samples with chemicals to remove possible contaminants. Knowing that small concentrations of collagen can attract contamination, they compared precision Accelerator Mass Spectrometry (AMS) tests of collagen and bioapatite (hard carbonate bone mineral) with conventional counting methods of large bone fragments from the same dinosaurs. "Comparing such different molecules as minerals and organics from the same bone region, we obtained concordant C-14 results which were well below the upper limits of C-14 dating. These, together with many other remarkable concordances between samples from different fossils, geographic regions and stratigraphic positions make random contamination as origin of the C-14 unlikely." John Michael Fischer, "Carbon-14-dated Dinosaur Bones are Less than 40,000 Years Old," *New Geology*, March 2020, https://newgeology.us/presentation48.html

The article goes on to discuss controversy regarding the above presentation. The research was rejected by the president of the Asia Oceania Geoscience Society after members complained that something had to be wrong, as in using conventional dating methods—that is, dating the fossils by the surrounding rocks, scientists had determined that the bone should be millions of years old. Similar discoveries were made by Mary Higby Schweitzer, PhD, a paleontologist at North Carolina State University, when she and her team were able to discover soft tissue within a tyrannosaurus bone which she received from a museum. Her discovery is controversial:

"The evidence, which she has laid out in a series of papers in *Science* and other journals, challenges traditional notions of what a fossil is: a stone replica of the original bone. If that 'stone' includes proteins from the living animal, 'I don't know what the definition is anymore,' Schweitzer says."

Robert Service, "I Don't Care What They Say About Me–Paleontologist Stares Down Her Critics in Her Hunt for Dinosaur Proteins," *Science*, September 13, 2017, https://www.sciencemag.org/news/2017/09/i-don-

t-care-what-they-say-about-me-paleontologist-
stares-down-critics-her-hunt/

"Mark Armitage, a published scientist of over 30 years, was working at the Hell Creek Formation excavation site in Montana when he discovered one of the largest Triceratops horns ever unearthed at the site. According to conventional perspectives, the Triceratops is a genus of herbivorous dinosaur that first appeared in the late Cretaceous period, about 68 million years ago in what is now North America, and became extinct around 66 million years ago. Armitage studied the fossil in the California State University lab using a high-powered microscope and was stunned to find soft tissue complete with bone cells. According to Armitage, the preservation of such cells is a scientific impossibility if the dinosaur really walked the earth over 66 million years ago. On this basis, he felt it was not unreasonable to open discussion with colleagues and students about the implications of such a finding being that the creationist perspective is correct and that dinosaurs existed much later than mainstream science maintains. The results of Armitage's analysis of the soft tissue was eventually published in July 2013 in the journal *Acta Histochemica.* Nevertheless, Armitage was fired from the University of California, which he is now fighting in court." *

April Holloway, "Scientist Dismissed After Soft Tissue Found on Dinosaur Fossil," *Ancient Origins,* July 25, 2014, https://www.ancient-origins.net/news-evolution-human-origins/scientist-dismissed-after-soft-tissue-found-dinosaur-fossil-001906

In 2016 Mark Armitage won a wrongful termination settlement of $399,500 from California State University. The university claimed the settlement was not an admission of guilt.

The implications of the above three studies are enormous; keep in mind that scientists have used the supposed ages of fossils to date the rocks in which they have been found—rocks which have been dated as millions of years old.

In 1997 a team of seven PhD scientists who believe in a young earth embarked on a project to investigate the methodologies from which the multi-billion-year age for the earth is derived. This became an eight-year study known as Radioisotopes and the Age of the Earth" (RATE), published in an 800-page report.

The team identified multiple independent lines of radioisotope evidence that the earth is merely thousands, rather than billions, years old, and evidence that nuclear decay rates have varied dramatically over time.

"The study deemed the most significant in support of this conclusion was the one that measured the diffusion (or migration) rate of helium in zircon crystals. This research found that the experimentally determined helium diffusion rate permits the high levels of helium measured in the zircons to persist no more than about 6,000 years. The helium in the zircons is the product of nuclear decay of uranium and its daughter products. This very short age is in stark conflict with the 1.5-billion-year age for these zircons provided by uranium-lead methods that assume time-invariant rates of nuclear decay. This short age result based on helium diffusion rates was supported by findings from two other RATE studies, one on the phenomenon of polonium radiohalos and the other on the ubiquitous presence of C-14 in organic materials dated by conventional radioisotope methods at millions to hundreds of millions of years."
John Baumgardner, PhD, "Radioisotopes and the

Age of the Earth," *Global Flood*, 2017, https://www.globalflood.org/radioisotopes.html

Scientists have observed that the earth's magnetic field is shifting and decaying—the pattern is consistent with the hypothesis that the magnetic field emanates from the earth's core, which is cooling down. This free-decay theory indicates that the earth's magnetic field would very likely be less than 10,000 years old.

"The average 'intensity' of the earth's magnetic field has decreased exponentially by about 7% since its first careful measurement in 1829. The field's intensity includes components of strength and direction and tells us the amount of force turning a compass needle northward. By estimating the field intensity everywhere (in, on, and above the earth), we can calculate the total electrical "energy" stored in the field. Such calculations show that the total energy in the field has decreased by about 14% since 1829." D. Russell Humphreys, PhD, "The Earth's Magnetic Field is Young," *Acts and Facts*, August 1, 1993, https://www.icr.org/article/371/

Creationists are of the opinion that the oil found in the ground is the result the rapid burial of plants and animals within sedimentary rock during the great flood. However, evolutionists claim that the fossil fuels developed over millions of years. Scientists have developed a lab process which enables them to turn sewage into biofuels within minutes.

In HTL [HydroThermal Liquefaction], the raw sewage is placed in a reactor that's basically a tube pressurized to 3,000 lb/in^2 (204 atm) and heated to 660° F (349° C), which mimics the same geological process that turned prehistoric organic matter into crude oil by breaking it down into simple compounds, only with HTL it takes minutes instead of epochs.
David Szondy, "Mimicking Nature Turns Sewage into Biocrude Oil in Minutes." *New Atlas*, November 3, 2016

Apparently there are several methodologies that evolutionary scientists use to calculate the age of the earth—all depend on pre-determined assumptions. Widely held theories are currently being challenged by scientific observations which do not fit mainstream explanations. A global flood would have caused some of the phenomena which evolutionary science attributes to other factors. Real science is based on evidence and full disclosure.

Conclusion

Hopefully, reading this booklet has aroused your curiosity such that you may wish to explore the subject of special creation/intelligent design on your own. I would especially encourage you to read through the books and articles mentioned in the bibliography. *Signature in the Cell* by Stephen Meyer is a thick book, but it is packed with well-researched information. I also would recommend *The Natural Limits to Biological Change* by Lane P. Lester and Raymond G. Bohlin. *Darwin's Racists*, written by Sharon Sebastian and Raymond G. Bohlin, is important in presenting the cultural/political climate in which Darwin's theory was embraced, and the consequences which resulted from that. Particularly helpful and informative is the web page for the book, *In the Beginning*, authored by Walt Brown (https://www.creationscience.com). Other creation science websites include, *Answers in Genesis* (https://answersingenesis.org), *Creation Ministries International*, (https://creation.com), *Discovery Institute* (https://www.discovery.org), and the *Institute for Creation Research* (https://www.icr.org).

The book of Job is perhaps the oldest book in the Bible. Noteworthy is the fact that scientists have found human footprints alongside those of the dinosaur (behemoth). Remember that reptiles continue to grow throughout their lives. Also consider the fact a worldwide flood vastly changed the world from its pre-flood conditions. Interesting verses to conclude this booklet are found in Job 40:15-24:

[15] "Look at Behemoth,
    which I made along with you
    and which feeds on grass like an ox.
[16] What strength it has in its loins,
    what power in the muscles of its belly!
[17] Its tail sways like a cedar;
    the sinews of its thighs are close-knit.
[18] Its bones are tubes of bronze,
    its limbs like rods of iron.
[19] It ranks first among the works of God,
    yet its Maker can approach it with his sword.
[20] The hills bring it their produce,
    and all the wild animals play nearby.
[21] Under the lotus plants it lies,
    hidden among the reeds in the marsh.
[22] The lotuses conceal it in their shadow;
    the poplars by the stream surround it.

²³ A raging river does not alarm it;
   it is secure, though the Jordan should
surge against its mouth.
²⁴ Can anyone capture it by the eyes,
   or trap it and pierce its nose?

I think about the monarch butterflies—their migration from Canada to Mexico where they winter and lay their eggs—and the caterpillars which go into a liquid state and emerge as butterflies that migrate back north to repeat the process. I think about the birds that build their nests with no instruction; the honeybees that communicate to one another through dance. How is it that we can navigate by the stars and the planets move with predictability such that we can clock time and seasons? There is so much that is too amazing for me to comprehend! Appreciate the wisdom and poetry found in Job 38-39:

38 Then the LORD spoke to Job out of the storm. He said:

² "Who is this that obscures My plans
   with words without knowledge?
³ Brace yourself like a man;

I will question you,
and you shall answer Me.

4 "Where were you when I laid the earth's
foundation?
     Tell Me, if you understand.
5 Who marked off its dimensions? Surely
you know!
     Who stretched a measuring line across
it?
6 On what were its footings set,
     or who laid its cornerstone—
7 while the morning stars sang together
     and all the angels shouted for joy?

8 "Who shut up the sea behind doors
     when it burst forth from the womb,
9 when I made the clouds its garment
     and wrapped it in thick darkness,
10 when I fixed limits for it
     and set its doors and bars in place,
11 when I said, 'This far you may come
and no farther;
     here is where your proud waves halt'?

12 "Have you ever given orders to the
morning,
     or shown the dawn its place,

¹³ that it might take the earth by the edges
  and shake the wicked out of it?
¹⁴ The earth takes shape like clay under a seal;
  its features stand out like those of a garment.
¹⁵ The wicked are denied their light,
  and their upraised arm is broken.
¹⁶ "Have you journeyed to the springs of the sea
  or walked in the recesses of the deep?
¹⁷ Have the gates of death been shown to you?
  Have you seen the gates of the deepest darkness?
¹⁸ Have you comprehended the vast expanses of the earth?
  Tell Me, if you know all this.

¹⁹ "What is the way to the abode of light?
  And where does darkness reside?
²⁰ Can you take them to their places?
  Do you know the paths to their dwellings?
²¹ Surely you know, for you were already born!
  You have lived so many years!

22 "Have you entered the storehouses of the snow
   or seen the storehouses of the hail,
23 which I reserve for times of trouble,
   for days of war and battle?
24 What is the way to the place where the lightning is dispersed,
   or the place where the east winds are scattered over the earth?
25 Who cuts a channel for the torrents of rain,
   and a path for the thunderstorm,
26 to water a land where no one lives,
   an uninhabited desert,
27 to satisfy a desolate wasteland
   and make it sprout with grass?
28 Does the rain have a father?
   Who fathers the drops of dew?
29 From whose womb comes the ice?
   Who gives birth to the frost from the heavens
30 when the waters become hard as stone,
   when the surface of the deep is frozen?

31 "Can you bind the chains of the Pleiades?

Can you loosen Orion's belt?
32 Can you bring forth the constellations in their seasons
   or lead out the Bear with its cubs?
33 Do you know the laws of the heavens?
   Can you set up God's dominion over the earth?

34 "Can you raise your voice to the clouds
   and cover yourself with a flood of water?
35 Do you send the lightning bolts on their way?
   Do they report to you, 'Here we are'?
36 Who gives the ibis wisdom
   or gives the rooster understanding?

37 Who has the wisdom to count the clouds?
   Who can tip over the water jars of the heavens
38 when the dust becomes hard
   and the clods of earth stick together?

39 "Do you hunt the prey for the lioness
   and satisfy the hunger of the lions
40 when they crouch in their dens
   or lie in wait in a thicket?

⁴¹ Who provides food for the raven
  when its young cry out to God
  and wander about for lack of food?

39 "Do you know when the mountain
goats give birth?
  Do you watch when the doe bears her
fawn?
² Do you count the months till they bear?
  Do you know the time they give birth?
³ They crouch down and bring forth their
young;
  their labor pains are ended.
⁴ Their young thrive and grow strong in
the wilds;
  they leave and do not return.

⁵ "Who let the wild donkey go free?
  Who untied its ropes?
⁶ I gave it the wasteland as its home,
  the salt flats as its habitat.
⁷ It laughs at the commotion in the town;
  it does not hear a driver's shout.
⁸ It ranges the hills for its pasture
  and searches for any green thing.

⁹ "Will the wild ox consent to serve you?
  Will it stay by your manger at night?

¹⁰ Can you hold it to the furrow with a harness?
　Will it till the valleys behind you?
¹¹ Will you rely on it for its great strength?
　Will you leave your heavy work to it?
¹² Can you trust it to haul in your grain
　and bring it to your threshing floor?

¹³ "The wings of the ostrich flap joyfully,
　though they cannot compare
　with the wings and feathers of the stork.
¹⁴ She lays her eggs on the ground
　and lets them warm in the sand,
¹⁵ unmindful that a foot may crush them,
　that some wild animal may trample them.
¹⁶ She treats her young harshly, as if they were not hers;
　she cares not that her labor was in vain,
¹⁷ for God did not endow her with wisdom
　or give her a share of good sense.
¹⁸ Yet when she spreads her feathers to run,
　she laughs at horse and rider.

[19] "Do you give the horse its strength
   or clothe its neck with a flowing mane?
[20] Do you make it leap like a locust,
   striking terror with its proud snorting?
[21] It paws fiercely, rejoicing in its strength,
   and charges into the fray.
[22] It laughs at fear, afraid of nothing;
   it does not shy away from the sword.
[23] The quiver rattles against its side,
   along with the flashing spear and lance.
[24] In frenzied excitement it eats up the ground;
   it cannot stand still when the trumpet sounds.
[25] At the blast of the trumpet it snorts, 'Aha!'
   It catches the scent of battle from afar,
   the shout of commanders and the battle cry.

[26] "Does the hawk take flight by your wisdom
   and spread its wings toward the south?
[27] Does the eagle soar at your command

and build its nest on high?
28 It dwells on a cliff and stays there at night;
a rocky crag is its stronghold.
29 From there it looks for food;
its eyes detect it from afar.
30 Its young ones feast on blood,
and where the slain are, there it is."

Bibliography

Books:

Behe, Michael J., *Darwin's Black Box*, Simon & Schuster, 2006

Berlinski, David, *The Devil's Delusion*, Basic Books, 2009

Brown, Walt, *In the Beginning, 8th Edition,* 2008
www.creationscience.com

Crick, Francis, *Life Itself—Its Origin and Nature*, Simon & Schuster, 1981

Fix, William R., *The Bone Peddlers*, McMillan Publishing Company, 1984

Gish, Duane T., *Evolution: The Fossils Still Say No!*, Institute for Creation Research, 1995

Lester, Lane P. & Bohlin, Raymond G., *The Natural Limits to Biological Change*, Probe Books 1989

Lewin, Roger, *Bones of Contention (Controversies in the Search for Human Origins)*, The University of Chicago Press, 1987

Lubenow, Marvin L., *Bones of Contention (A Creationist Assessment of Human Fossils)*, Baker Publishing Company, 2004

Meyer, Stephen C., *Signature in the Cell*, Harper Collins Publishers, 2009

Sebastian, Sharon & Bohlin, Raymond G., *Darwin's Racists*, VBW Publishing, 2009

Simmons, Geoffrey, *What Darwin Didn't Know*, Harvest House, 2004

Smith, Wolfgang, *Teilhardism and the New Religion: A Thorough Analysis of the Teachings of de Chardin*, Tan Books & Publishers, 1988

Sunderland, Luther D., *Darwin's Enigma*, Master Book Publishers, 1988

Wells, Jonathan, *Icons of Evolution*, Regnery Publishing, 2002

Articles:

Alper, Joe, "Rethinking Neanderthals," *Smithsonian Magazine*, June 2003, Vol. 34, Iss. 3, p. 82, https://www.smithsonianmag.com/science-nature/rethinking-neanderthals-83341003/

Baumgardner, John, "Radioisotopes and the Age of the Earth," *Global Flood*, 2017, https://www.globalflood.org/radioisotopes.html

Bergman, Jerry, "The Ape-to-Human progression: The Most Common Evolution Icon is a Fraud," Journal of Creation, March 23, 2009, https://creation.com/images/pdfs/tj/j23_3/j23_3_1 6-20.pdf

Callaway, Ewen, "Genetic Adam and Eve Did Not Live Too Far Apart in Time," *Nature News*, August 6, 2013, https://www.nature.com/news

Caramelli, David et al, "Europe's Ancestors: Cro-Magnon 28,000 Years Old Had DNA Like Modern Humans," *Science Daily*, July 16, 2008, https://www.sciencedaily.com/releases/2008/07/0 80715204741.htm

Durston, Kirk "Microevolution Versus Macroevolution: Two Mistakes," *Evolution News and Science Today*, July 16, 2015, https://evolutionnews.org//2015/07/microevolution/

Gee, Henry, "Paleoanthropology: Craniums with Clout," *Nature*, October 5, 2011, https://www.nature.com/articles/478034a

Gibbons, Ann, "Calibrating the Mitochondrial Clock," *Science*, January 2, 1998, Vol. 279, p. 29, http://www.dnai.org/teacherguide/pdf/reference_r omanovs.pdf

Harris, Karen, "Our Image of Neanderthals is All Wrong: The First Skeleton was Arthritic," *Ancient History*, August 20, 2019, https://historydaily.org/our-image-of-neanderthals-is-all-wrong-the-first-skeleton-was-arthritic

Haskett, Dorothy L., "Mitochondrial DNA and Human Evolution," *The Embryo Project Encyclopedia*, October 10, 2014, https://embryo.asu.edu/pages/mitochondrial-dna-and-human-evolution-1987-rebecca-louise-cann-mark-stoneking-and-allan

Henderson, Doug, "Bringing Lucy to Life," *Answers Magazine*, January 1, 2013, https://answersingenesis.org/human-evolution/lucy/bringing"-lucy-to-life/

Hirst, K. Kris, "Why Don't We Call them Cro-Magnon Anymore?," *Thought Co.*, November 14, 2019, https://www.thoughtco.com/we-dont-call-them-cro-magnon-170738

Holloway, April, "Scientist Dismissed After Soft Tissue Found on Dinosaur Fossil," *Ancient Origins*, July 25, 2014, https://www.ancient-origins.net/news-evolution-human-origins/scientist-dismissed-after-soft-tissue-found-dinosaur-fossil-001906

Humphreys, D. Russell, "The Earth's Magnetic Field is Young," *Acts and Facts*, August 1, 1993, https://www.icr.org/article/371/

Jablonski, Nina G. and Chaplin, George, "Human Skin Pigmentation as an Adaptation to UV Radiation," *Proceedings of the National Academy of Scientists,* May 11, 2010, p. 107, https://www.pnas.org/content/107/Supplement_2/8962

Jeanson, Nathaniel T., PhD, and Holland, Ashley D., "Evidence for a Human Y Chromosome Molecular Clock: Pedigree-Based Mutation Rates Suggest a 4,500-Year History for Human Paternal Inheritance," *Answers Research Journal,* December 4, 2019, https://answersingenesis.org/theory-of-evolution/molecular-clock/evidence-human-y-chromosome-molecular-clock/

Mehlert, A. W., "Homo Erectus 'to' Modern Man: Evolution or Human Variability?," *Journal of Creation,* https://creation.com/homo-erectus-to-modern-man-evolution-or-human-variability

Miller, Jeff, PhD, "21 Reasons to Believe the Earth is Young," *Apologetics Press,* http://apologeticspress.org/APContent.aspx?catego ry=9&article=5641

Mitchell, Elizabeth, "What Can Lucy's Neighbors Tell Us About Human Origins?," *Answers in Genesis*, June 9, 2015, https://answersingenesis.org/human-evolution/ape-man/what-can-lucys-neighbors-tell-us-about-human-origins/

Parsons, Thomas J., PhD, et al., "A High Observed Substitution Rate in the Human Mitochondrial DNA Control Region," *Nature Genetics*, April 1997, Vol. 15, p. 365, https://www.nature.com/articles/ng0497-363

Patterson, Roger, "Dating Methods," *Answers in Genesis*, January 6, 2011, https://answersingenesis.org/age-of-the-earth/dating-methods/

Pruitt, Sarah, "Piltdown Man Hoax," *History*, December 18, 2012, https://www.history.com/news/piltdown-man-hoax-100-years-ago

Redman, Samuel, "What the Piltdown Man Hoax from 1912 Can Teach Science Today," *The Conversation,* U Mass Amherst, May 4, 2017, https://theconversation.com/behind-closed-doors-what-the-piltdown-man-hoax-from-1912-can-teach-science-today-76967

Science Daily, "Europe's Ancestors: Cro-Magnon 28,000 Years Old Had DNA Like Modern Humans," *Science News*, July 16, 2008, https://www.sciencedaily.com/releases/2008/07/080715204741.htm

Scoville, Heather, "Nebraska Man–An Evolution Hoax," *ThoughtCo*, January 27, 2020, https://www.thoughtco.com/nebraska-man-1224737

Service, Robert, "I Don't Care What They Say About Me–Paleontologist Stares Down Her Critics in Her Hunt for Dinosaur Proteins," *Science*, September 13, 2017, https://www.sciencemag.org/news/2017/09/i-don-t-care-what-they-say-about-me-paleontologist-stares-down-critics-her-hunt/

Sherwin, Frank, "Lucy Languishes as a Human-Ape Link," *Acts and Facts*, April 28, 2017, https://www.icr.org/article/lucy-languishes-human-ape-link/

Szondy, David, "Mimicking Nature Turns Sewage into Biocrude Oil in Minutes," *New Atlas*, November 3, 2016

Switeg, Brian, "The Truth About the Nebraska Man," *Science Blogs*, February 21, 2008, https://scienceblogs.com/laelaps/2008/02/21/the-truth-about-nebraska-man

Tayag, Yasmin, "Neanderthal Study Corrects "Absurd" Misconception About Hunch," *Inverse*, February 25, 2019, https://www.inverse.com/article/53560-neanderthals-weren-t-hunched-over-they-walked-upright

Thomas, Brian PhD, "Who Were Cro-Magnon People?," *Acts and Facts*, November 30, 2017, https://www.icr.org/article/who-were-cro-magnon-people

Tomkins, Jeffrey P., "The Impossibility of Life's Evolutionary Beginnings," *Acts and Facts*, February 28, 2018, https://www.icr.org/article/impossibility-lifes-evolutionary-beginnings

Wald, George. "The Origin Of Life," *Scientific American*, August, 1954, Vol. 191, No. 2, https://www.jstor.org/stable/e24943585

Weidenbach, Kristin, "Why Study the Y: Chromosome Reveals Path of Ancestral Humans," *Stanford Report*, November 8, 2000, https://news.stanford.edu/news/2000/november8/chromosome-1108.html

Wieland, Carl, "Who Was Java Man?," *Creation Ministries International*, June 1991, pp. 22-23, https://creation.com/who-was-java-man

Wells, Jonathan, "Homology in Biology, A Problem for Naturalistic Science," *The True Origin* Archive, April 21, 2020, https://trueorigin.org/homology.php

Wieland, Carl, "Who Was Java Man?," *Creation Ministries International*, June 1991, pp. 22-23, https://creation.com/who-was-java-man

Wolf, John and Mellett, James, "The Role of the Nebraska Man in the Creation/Evolution Debate," *Creation/Evolution Journal,* Summer 1985, Vol. 5, No. 2, https://ncse.ngo/role-nebraska-man-creation-evolution-debate

Made in the USA
Columbia, SC
30 August 2024

40831266R00064